4.4

D1266097

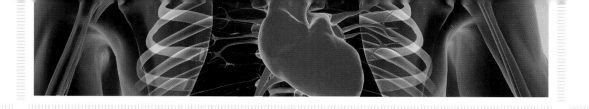

TAKE A CLOSER LOOK AT YOUR
Heart

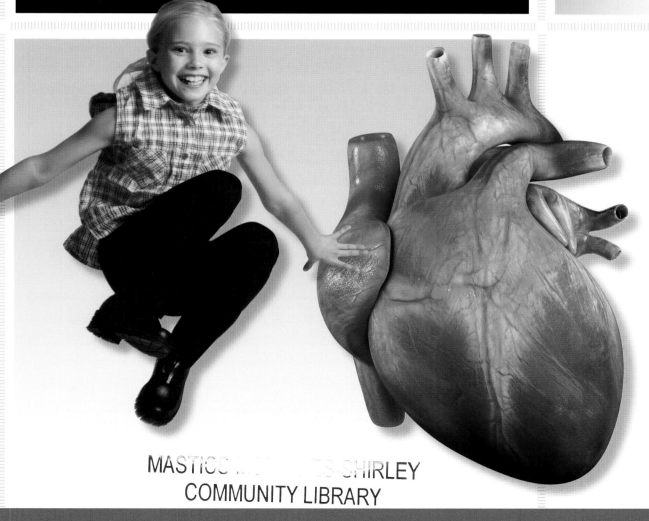

BY JANET SLIKE

The Child's World

Published by The Child's World®
1980 Lookout Drive • Mankato, MN 56003-1705
800-599-READ • www.childsworld.com

Acknowledgments
The Child's World®: Mary Berendes, Publishing Director
Red Line Editorial: Editorial direction and production
The Design Lab: Design
Content Consultant: Jeffrey W. Oseid, MD

Photographs ©: Photodisc, 4, 23; Levente Győri/
iStockphoto, 5, 24; Gunnar Assmy/Shutterstock Images, 7;
Shutterstock Images, 8, 9, 10, 17; Monkey Business Images/
Shutterstock Images, 13, 21; Tyler Olson/Shutterstock
Images, 15; Alila Sao Mai/Shutterstock Images, 16;
John Wollwerth/Shutterstock Images, 18; Morgan Lane
Photography/Shutterstock Images, 19

Front cover: Shutterstock Images; Photodisc; Gunnar Assmy/
Shutterstock Images

ISBN: 978-1623235475
LCCN: 2013931457

Printed in the United States of America
Mankato, MN
July, 2013
PA02175

About the Author

Janet Slike is a freelance editor and writer. Her short stories for adults have appeared in the anthology *Columbus: Past, Present, Future* and several magazines. Her interest in the heart comes from personal experience. She is proud to be a heart attack survivor.

Table of Contents

CHAPTER 1

In a Heartbeat

Did you know you own something that pumps 2,000 gallons (7,570 l) of fluid a day? Of course, you don't have a gas station pump in your bedroom. But you do have a heart in the center of your chest. Your heart is an amazing organ that pumps blood to your whole body. Blood has the **nutrients** your organs need to work.

You can feel how fast your heart is pumping blood. Place your fingers on the side of your throat just under your chin to feel your **pulse**.

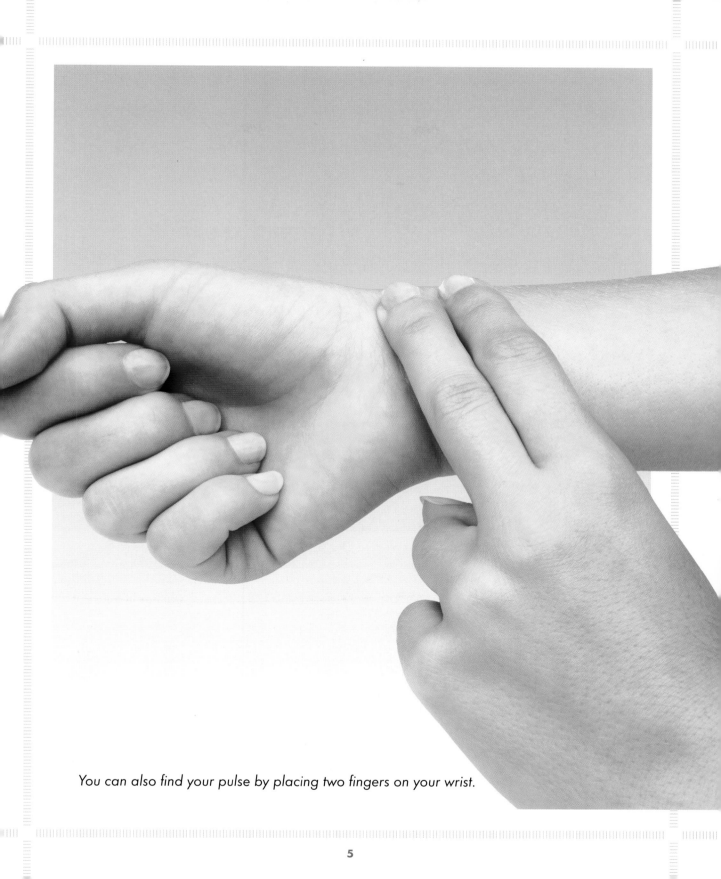

You can also find your pulse by placing two fingers on your wrist.

The heart is a muscle in the **circulatory system**. It doesn't look like the hearts you see on a Valentine's Day card. It is shaped like a pear with tubes attached. A baby's heart is the size of his or her fist. As you grow, your heart grows, too. Your heart will always be the size of your fist.

A woman's heart weighs about 8 ounces (227 g). A man's heart weighs about 10 ounces (283 g). The heart is small but powerful. Do you have a squirt gun? Some squirt guns can squirt water a few feet or yards. But your heart can squirt blood 30 feet (9 m) if an **artery** is cut. This power helps blood travel through your body.

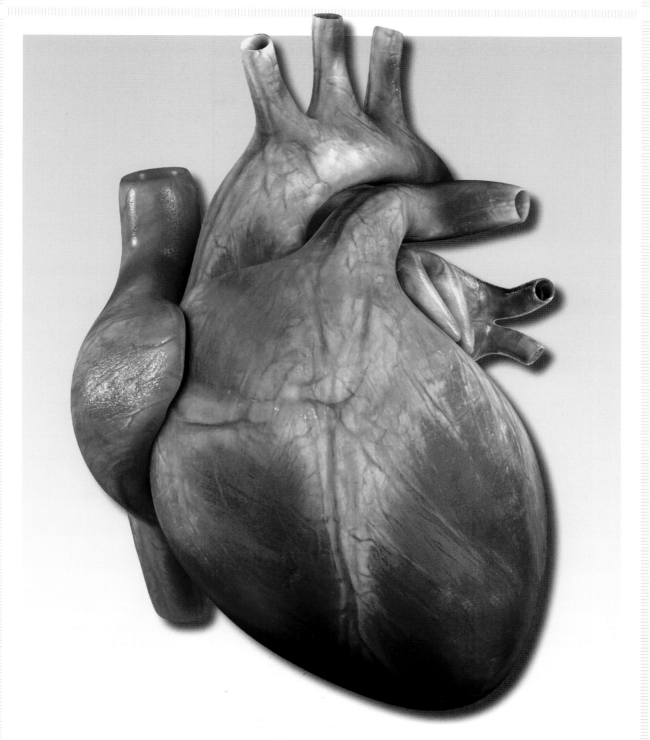

A human heart looks much different than the hearts you draw on paper.

CHAPTER 2

How Does the Heart Work?

The heart has four parts called chambers. The top two chambers are called atria. Each top chamber is called an **atrium**. An atrium collects blood. The two bottom chambers are called **ventricles**. A ventricle pumps blood.

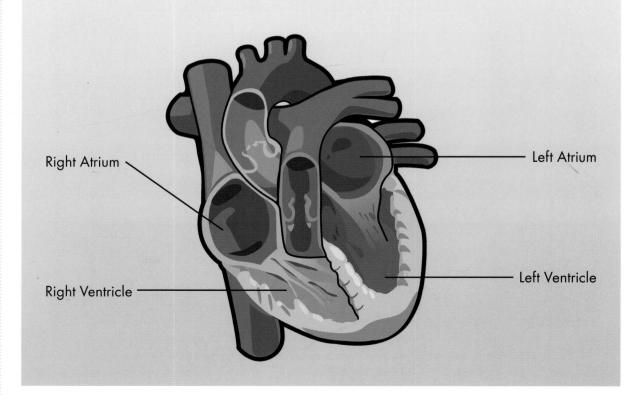

Right Atrium

Left Atrium

Right Ventricle

Left Ventricle

The right ventricle pumps blood to the lungs. At the same time, the left ventricle pumps blood to the rest of the body. Each side picks up blood and delivers it. A single blood cell travels through your body in just 20 seconds. The right atrium collects the blood that has **carbon dioxide**. This blood doesn't have much oxygen. The right ventricle pumps this blood to the lungs to get oxygen.

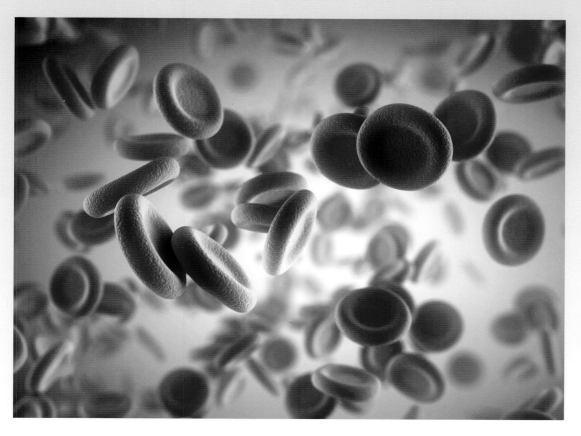

The left ventricle pumps blood cells through the entire body.

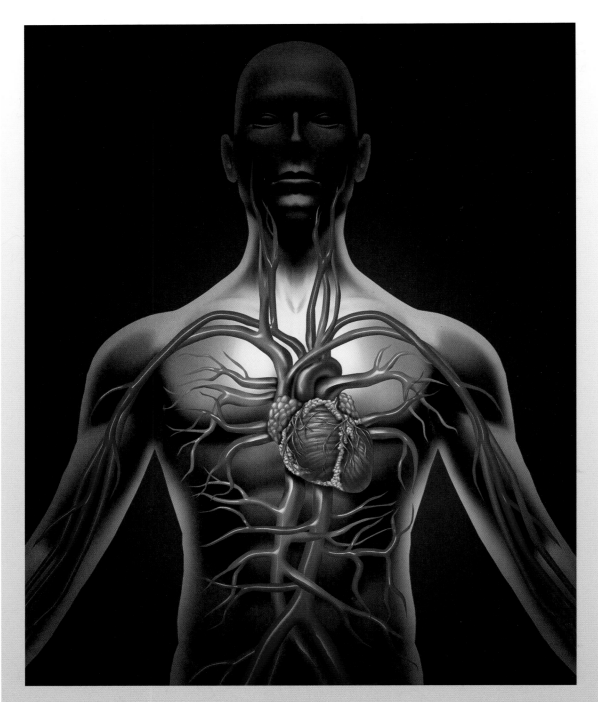

Blood from the heart is shown in red, while blood going to the lungs is shown in blue.

Blood is pumped through **veins** and arteries. Veins carry blood to the heart. Arteries carry blood away from the heart. You can remember this easily because "arteries" and "away" both start with "a." The smallest arteries are **capillaries**. One strand of human hair is ten times wider than some capillaries.

The veins, arteries, and capillaries take up a lot of space in your body. You have 60,000 miles (96, 561 km) of them. If you place them end to end, they would circle Earth twice!

Once the arteries carry the blood to the lungs, the lungs remove the blood's carbon dioxide and waste products. Then the lungs add oxygen to the blood. This blood goes to the left atrium, then to the left ventricle. The left ventricle pumps it out to the body. Both sides pump at the same time.

CHAPTER 3

Who Needs a Heart?

Everyone needs a heart. Long ago, people thought the heart was what made us happy or sad. But the heart plays a more important role. It keeps us alive. The heart controls blood flow. So it is very important. The heart makes sure all of your organs get the blood and oxygen they need. Without blood, organs can't perform their jobs.

Make a fist. Open it a little. Make it again. Your heart moves like this 100,000 times a day. Your heart doesn't stop pumping blood when you sleep. During sleep it slows down because your organs don't need as much oxygen.

The heart brings blood and oxygen to your organs so you can play your favorite sports.

When organs don't get enough blood, they fail. If the brain doesn't get oxygen from the blood, it suffers a stroke. Some parts of the brain die during a stroke. This means the brain can't always tell the body what to do. After a stroke, a person may have trouble walking or talking.

Doctors sometimes use robots to help with heart surgeries. Doctors control the robot hands with a remote. Robot hands can make smaller and better cuts than human hands.

You can't live without a heart. But some people live with hearts they weren't born with. When a heart can't be fixed, doctors can put in an artificial heart. Or they can do a heart transplant. Dr. Christiaan Barnard did the first heart transplant in 1967.

After a stroke, a person might have to learn how to walk again.

CHAPTER 4

Broken Hearts

Since the heart does so much work, things can sometimes go wrong. Your heart has four **valves**. Each time your heart beats, the valves open and close. They do this two at a time. The valves are like gates. They make sure blood only flows one way.

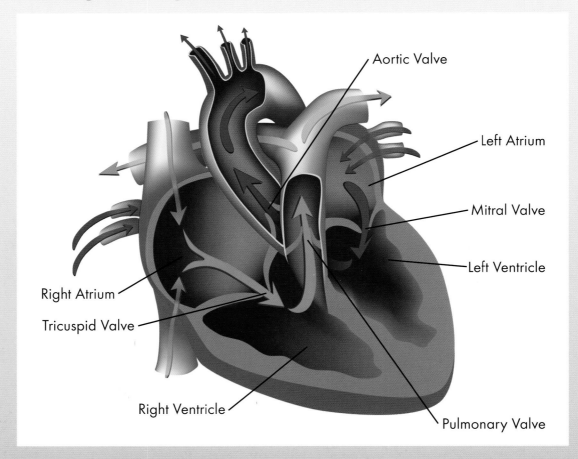

Aortic Valve

Left Atrium

Mitral Valve

Left Ventricle

Right Atrium

Tricuspid Valve

Right Ventricle

Pulmonary Valve

When a car goes the wrong way down the street, it is dangerous. Blood going the wrong way is dangerous, too. A heart murmur occurs when some blood moves backward.

An artery can get completely blocked, or clogged. If blood can't flow through it, the person has what is called a heart attack. When a person has a heart attack, he or she must go to the hospital. Doctors can do surgery to make the blood take a different path to the heart. This is called **bypass** surgery.

A pig valve can replace a human valve. Pig valves are similar enough to human valves to work just fine.

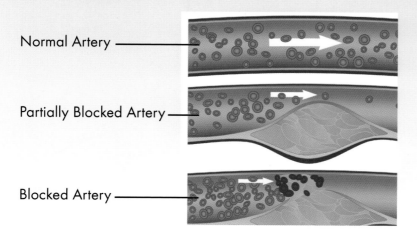

Normal Artery

Partially Blocked Artery

Blocked Artery

A clogged artery makes it difficult for blood to flow to your organs properly.

CHAPTER 5

Heart Healthy

You can help keep your heart healthy. One way to help is to be active. Exercise that keeps your body moving and your heart pumping hard is the best. Exercise does not make your heart tired. It makes it stronger. Biking, running, and dancing are all good activities that exercise your heart.

Swimming is a great way to exercise your heart.

What you eat affects your heart. Eat at least five servings of fruits and vegetables every day. Grains should also be eaten daily. Grains lower **cholesterol** in your blood. Your body needs cholesterol to build cell walls, digest food, and absorb vitamins. But too much cholesterol can clog your arteries.

Breads and pastas are good grains to eat to help keep your heart healthy.

Foods with too much salt or fat are not good for your heart. Salty foods can raise your blood pressure. Fatty foods can raise your cholesterol and make you gain too much weight. Extra weight makes it harder for your heart to pump blood.

Stress can be dangerous for your heart. Try to not let things bother you. Do something relaxing every day. Laugh often. Laughing can keep stress levels down, which is good for your heart. So it's healthy to share jokes with your friends. Your heart works hard so every part of your body can function. Treat it well, and keep it pumping!

Playing and laughing with friends is fun and good for your heart!

artery (AHR-tur-ee) An artery is one of the tubes that carries blood away from the heart. Arteries carry blood from your heart to the rest of your body.

atrium (AY-tree-uhm) An atrium is one of the two upper chambers of the heart. Each atrium collects blood for the heart to pump.

bypass (BYE-pas) To bypass means to take a different path. Heart bypass surgery changes the path by which blood flows.

capillaries (KAP-uh-ler-eez) Capillaries are very small tubes that carry blood. Capillaries are the smallest kinds of arteries.

carbon dioxide (KAHR-buhn dye-AHK-side) Carbon dioxide is a gas made up of carbon and oxygen. The lungs remove carbon dioxide from blood.

cholesterol (kuh-LES-tuh-rawl) Cholesterol is a fatty substance in the blood. Too much cholesterol in the blood can cause heart problems.

circulatory system (SUR-kyuh-luh-tor-ee SIS-tuhm) The organs that pump blood through the body make up the circulatory system. The heart, veins, and arteries are all part of the circulatory system.

nutrients (NOO-tree-uhnts) Nutrients are minerals or vitamins the body needs to stay strong and healthy. Blood brings nutrients to the organs.

pulse (puhls) A steady throb is called a pulse. The heart makes a pulse when the heart valves open and close.

valves (valvz) Valves control the way a liquid flows. Valves in the heart make sure blood flows the right way.

veins (vaynz) Veins are small tubes that run through the body. Veins carry blood back to the heart from other parts of the body.

ventricles (VEN-tri-kuhlz) The two bottom chambers of the heart are called ventricles. The ventricles pump blood to the lungs and other parts of the body.

LEARN MORE

BOOKS

Simon, Seymour. *The Heart: Our Circulatory System.* New York: Collins, 2006.

Stewart, Melissa. *Pump it Up!* New York: Marshall Cavendish Benchmark, 2010.

Walker, Richard. *The Heart in Action.* Mankato, MN: Smart Apple Media, 2005.

WEB SITES

Visit our Web site for links about the heart: **childsworld.com/links**

Note to Parents, Teachers, and Librarians: We routinely verify our Web links to make sure they are safe and active sites. So encourage your readers to check them out!

INDEX